This Book Belongs To

_____

_____

My Favourite Sticker

My Favourite Sticker

My Favourite Sticker

My Favourite Sticker

My Favourite Sticker

My Favourite Sticker

My Favourite Sticker

My Favourite Sticker

My Favourite Sticker

My Favourite Sticker

My Favourite Sticker

My Favourite Sticker

My Favourite Sticker

My Favourite Sticker

My Favourite Sticker

My Favourite Sticker

My Favourite Sticker

My Favourite Sticker

My Favourite Sticker

My Favourite Sticker

My Favourite Sticker

My Favourite Sticker

My Favourite Sticker

My Favourite Sticker

My Favourite Sticker

My Favourite Sticker

My Favourite Sticker

My Favourite Sticker

My Favourite Sticker

My Favourite Sticker

My Favourite Sticker

My Favourite Sticker

My Favourite Sticker

My Favourite Sticker

My Favourite Sticker

My Favourite Sticker

My Favourite Sticker

My Favourite Sticker

My Favourite Sticker

My Favourite Sticker

My Favourite Sticker

My Favourite Sticker

My Favourite Sticker

My Favourite Sticker

My Favourite Sticker

My Favourite Sticker

My Favourite Sticker

My Favourite Sticker

My Favourite Sticker

My Favourite Sticker

My Favourite Sticker

My Favourite Sticker

My Favourite Sticker

My Favourite Sticker

My Favourite Sticker

My Favourite Sticker

My Favourite Sticker

My Favourite Sticker

My Favourite Sticker

My Favourite Sticker

My Favourite Sticker

My Favourite Sticker

My Favourite Sticker

My Favourite Sticker

My Favourite Sticker

My Favourite Sticker

My Favourite Sticker

My Favourite Sticker

My Favourite Sticker

My Favourite Sticker

My Favourite Sticker

My Favourite Sticker

My Favourite Sticker

My Favourite Sticker

My Favourite Sticker

My Favourite Sticker

My Favourite Sticker

My Favourite Sticker

My Favourite Sticker

My Favourite Sticker

My Favourite Sticker

My Favourite Sticker

My Favourite Sticker

My Favourite Sticker

My Favourite Sticker

My Favourite Sticker

My Favourite Sticker

My Favourite Sticker

My Favourite Sticker

My Favourite Sticker

My Favourite Sticker

My Favourite Sticker

My Favourite Sticker

My Favourite Sticker

My Favourite Sticker

My Favourite Sticker

My Favourite Sticker

My Favourite Sticker

My Favourite Sticker

Made in the USA
Middletown, DE
30 November 2024

65683192R00057